English words that come from Arabic

admiral algebra almanac cipher

genie lute mosque syrup talc

Welcome to Egypt

Meredith Costain Paul Collins

MACMILLAN
LIBRARY

First published in 2002 by
MACMILLAN EDUCATION AUSTRALIA PTY LTD
627 Chapel Street, South Yarra 3141

Associated companies and representatives throughout the world.

National Library of Australia
Cataloguing-in-Publication Data

Costain, Meredith, 1955–.
        Welcome to Egypt.

        Includes index.
        ISBN 0 7329 7886 6.

        1. Egypt – Civilization – Juvenile literature.
        2. Egypt – Social life and customs – Juvenile literature.
        I. Collins, Paul, 1954–. II. Title. (Series: Macmillan countries).

372.8962

Edited by Miriana Dasovic
Text design by Goanna Graphics (Vic) Pty Ltd
Cover design by Goanna Graphics (Vic) Pty Ltd
Illustration by Vaughan Duck
Map by Stephen Pascoe

Printed in Hong Kong

Acknowledgements

The author and the publisher are grateful to the following for permission to reproduce copyright material:

Cover photograph: Sphinx at the Temple of Karnak, courtesy of Lonely Planet Images/Troy Flower.

AUSCAPE/© John Rainbird, p. 13 (bottom); Australian Picture Library/Bilderberg Archiv der Fotografi, p. 13 (top); Australian Picture Library/Corbis, p. 24; Australian Picture Library/David Ball, pp. 15 (bottom), 21 (top); Australian Picture Library/D & J Heaton, p. 22; Australian Picture Library/E T Archive, p. 29; Australian Picture Library/Jose Fuste Raga, p. 12; Australian Picture Library/J P & E S Bake, pp. 5, 30 (1st row); Australian Picture Library/Steve Vidler, p. 23 (top); Australian Picture Library/Universal Pictures, pp. 28, 30 (2nd row); Colin Sale/Atlas Picture Library, pp. 19 (top), 25 (bottom), 26, 30 (4th row: right & left, 5th row); Fred Adler/Kino Studios, pp. 8, 19 (bottom), 25 (top), 27 (bottom); Lonely Planet Images/Greg Elms, p. 9; Lonely Planet Images/John Borthwick, p. 15 (top); Lonely Planet Images/Juliet Coombe, pp. 6, 7 (both); Lonely Planet Images/Mark Webster, p. 21 (bottom); Lonely Planet Images/Leanne Logan, pp. 10, 18, 27 (top); Lonely Planet Images/Patrick Syder, p. 20; Lonely Planet Images/Thomas Hartwell, p. 14; Lonely Planet Images/Troy Flower, p. 23 (bottom); Patrick Horton, p. 11 (both), 30 (4th row: middle, 6th row).

While every care has been taken to trace and acknowledge copyright, the publishers tender their apologies for any accidental infringement where copyright has proved untraceable. Where the attempt has been unsuccessful, the publishers welcome information that would redress the situation.

Contents

	Page
Map of Egypt	4
Welcome to Egypt!	5
Family life	6
School	8
Sport and leisure	9
Egyptian culture	10
Festivals and religion	12
Food and shopping	14
Make hommos	16
Write a message with hieroglyphics	17
Landscape and climate	18
Plants and animals	20
Cities and landmarks	22
Industry and agriculture	24
Transport	26
History and government	28
Fact file	30
Glossary	31
Index	32

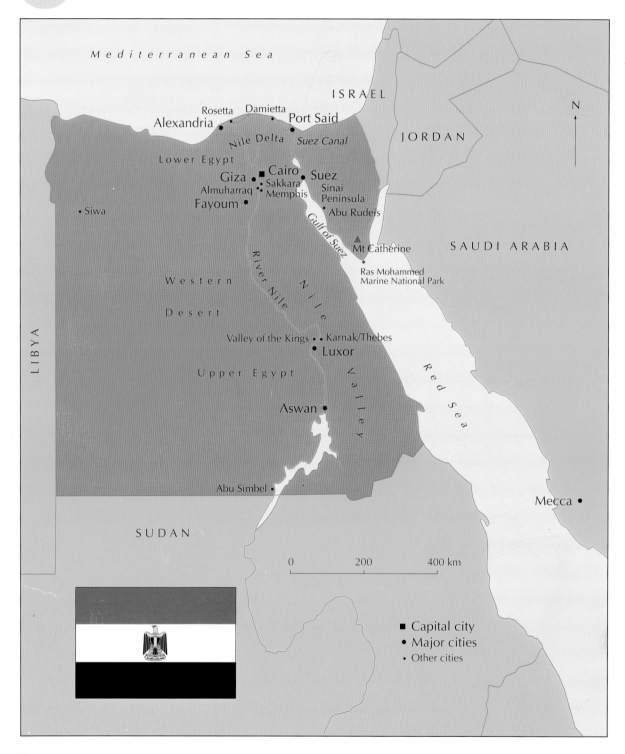

Mediterranean Sea

ISRAEL

JORDAN

N

Rosetta   Damietta
Alexandria   Port Said
Nile Delta   Suez Canal

Lower Egypt

Giza   Cairo   Suez
Sakkara   Sinai
Almuharraq   Memphis   Peninsula
Fayoum   Abu Rudeis

Siwa

SAUDI ARABIA

Mt Catherine

Ras Mohammed
Marine National Park

Western

Desert

Valley of the Kings   Karnak/Thebes
Luxor

Upper Egypt

Aswan

Red Sea

Abu Simbel

Mecca

SUDAN

LIBYA

River Nile

Nile   Valley

Gulf of Suez

0   200   400 km

■ Capital city
● Major cities
• Other cities

Welcome to Egypt!

Ahalan! My name is Mahmoud. I come from Siwa, an **oasis** town in the great Western Desert, in Egypt.

Egypt is the 12th-largest country in Africa, by area. Our neighbours are Libya to the west, Sudan to the south, and Israel and Jordan to the east. Saudi Arabia is on the other side of the Red Sea. The Nile is one of the greatest rivers in the world. It flows through our country and empties into the Mediterranean Sea. Although two-thirds of our country is covered in desert, the land around the Nile is rich and green.

Our country has one of the oldest cultures in the world. Every year, thousands of tourists come to visit our ancient pyramids, temples and tombs. They also take cruises on the River Nile, or try to solve the riddle of the Sphinx at Giza.

Our national language is Arabic, but many people speak English and French as well. In Siwa, we speak a **Berber** language known as Siwi. Our flag has three stripes. The black stripe stands for our dark past, the red stripe for the revolution, and the white stripe for our country's bright future. The gold hawk in the middle stands for Mohammed, the founder of **Islam**.

Family life

Siwa is in the north-west of Egypt, close to the Libyan border. The people here are a mixture of the Berber and **Bedouin** tribes. Our language, dress and many of our customs are different from those of the people living in big cities such as Cairo and Alexandria. The town is 18 metres below sea level, and grew up around an oasis. Without water, it would be impossible for people to survive in the desert.

My father, Omar, is a *zaggala*, which means 'stick-bearer'. There are many date palms around our town, and my father uses his stick to gather the dates. My mother, Safa, looks after the house and family. I have two sisters, Fatimah and Eisha, and a brother, Khalid. He helps my uncle at the camel-trading market.

My father and my sisters outside our house. The walls are made of thick mud, which helps to keep things cool inside.

My mother and sisters wash our clothes and dishes at the local well. Every village in Egypt has a well or fountain that provides clean, running water.

After school I play soccer in the streets with my friends. My sisters stay inside and help my mother with the cooking and housework. Fatimah is getting married soon. Many girls in Siwa are married by the time they are 14.

My brother, Khalid, and our cousins at the camel-trading market. When I am old enough, I will help out here too.

School

Egyptian children start school at the age of six, and must stay at school until they are 12. Many students then leave to either find a job, or help their parents at home or in the fields. After primary school, students can go on to study at either a general school, which prepares students for university, or a technical school, where they learn about farming and industry. There are also special institutes where you can study drama, ballet or film-making. I would love to make movies!

Classrooms in city schools can be very crowded, but my school is small. My subjects include Arabic, mathematics, science, religion and sport. We have lots of exams, which are very hard. At the end of primary school, we have a series of tests. These help decide which school we will move on to. But I will be leaving school once I turn 12, just as my brother did. Then I will help my uncle at the camel-trading market.

A group of boys learning lessons from the Koran, the sacred (holy) book of Islam. The first chapter of the book is recited by Muslims every day. This is part of their prayers.

Sport and leisure

Egyptian people love sport. Basketball and volleyball are popular, but soccer is the best! Whenever a big game is played at the national stadium in Cairo, the streets are deserted. Most people either watch the game at the stadium, dressed in club colours, or at home on TV. If their team wins a big match, they parade around in their cars, waving flags and tooting horns. I always watch the game at a neighbour's house. My favourite team is El Ahly.

People who live in cities on the coast, such as Alexandria, enjoy swimming and sunbaking. In Cairo, families get together for an evening picnic along the grassy banks of the Nile. On national holidays, local people sometimes take a day trip to the pyramids. There are thousands of overseas tourists doing the same thing!

In the evenings, after a hard day's work in the market or the fields, men gather at their local coffee house to relax. There they chat about politics or local events, or play cards, dominoes or shish bish *(backgammon). Women are more likely to gather with their friends in the courtyard of a private home.*

Egyptian culture

Egypt has had a thriving culture for over 4000 years. The ancient Egyptians painted their walls and pottery with scenes from daily life. Our most basic items, such as boxes, rugs, pots and pans, are still highly decorated. The materials used to make these items include gold, silver, brass and copper. Tiny pieces of **mother-of-pearl** are inlaid into wood to form mosaic patterns.

The ancient Egyptians composed beautiful songs and hymns, which they played on harps, lutes and flutes. These days, folk music is played on lutes, violas, tambourines, drums and fiddles. Classical music is played at religious ceremonies. Folk dances are performed at weddings and festivals. Our most famous dance is the belly dance, which is performed by women. Sometimes they dance with candles, so that people can admire the skill and grace of their movements.

A mural on the wall of the tomb of Nefertari in Luxor. Nefertari was the favourite wife of Ramses II, one of ancient Egypt's many kings. Ramses had five wives and 140 children.

Movie posters in Opera Square, Cairo. Egyptian movies and movie stars are very popular in Arab countries.

The ancient Egyptians also developed a form of writing known as hieroglyphics. These were used to write songs and poems, as well as legal and trade documents. Poetry is still popular in Egypt today. Our most famous writers include Taha Hussein, and Naguib Mahfouz – who won the Nobel Prize for Literature in 1988.

A gold jewellery shop in Cairo. Many villagers prefer to invest in chunky gold and silver jewellery rather than put their money in a bank.

Festivals and religion

The ancient Egyptians worshipped many gods, and believed in life after death. They built large tombs to protect the bodies of kings and queens, as well as their servants. These days there are two main religions in Egypt – Islam and Christianity.

Most Egyptians are Muslim. They believe there is only one god, Allah, and that Mohammed was his **prophet**. Muslims believe that they should live according to the rules of Islam. This way they will find peace with Allah, with each other, and with the world around them. At least once in their lives, many Muslim Egyptians aim to make a journey to **Mecca**. This journey is called the *hajj*. When they return to their villages, they paint scenes from their trip on the walls of their houses.

The Sultan Hassan Mosque in Cairo. Muslims are expected to pray five times a day, no matter where they are. They must kneel down and face Mecca. Women pray in a separate part of the mosque from men.

Morning prayer at the Coptic Orthodox Monastery of the Holy St Mary, in Almuharraq. Copts have their own pope and follow different religious holidays from other Christian religions.

Every year, Muslims observe the holy month of **Ramadan**. Adults and older children go without food or drink from dawn until sunset. It helps them to remember the poor people in the world who do not have enough to eat or drink. At the end of the month, they break their fast with a festival known as Id-ul-Fitr. They dress in their best clothes, eat special foods and give presents to their families.

A Sufi dancer in Cairo. People who follow the order of Sufi believe that they will find a way to God through love and devotion.

Egyptian festivals and holidays

New Year's Day	1 January
Christmas Day	7 January
Easter	March/April
National Day	23 July
Feast of Virgin Mary	15 August
Id ul-Fitr (end of Ramadan)*	
Id ul-Adha (Pilgrimage to Mecca)*	
Month of Muharram (New Year)*	
Birthday of the Prophet Mohammed*	

* These dates vary each year.

Food and shopping

Egyptian people love to eat! In the cities, people might have as many as five meals a day. Some of the meals may be only light snacks. Other meals might have lots of different courses, and can last for several hours.

A Bedouin family shares a meal. In country areas, meals are much simpler than in the city.

Breakfast is often a quick drink at home, topped off with some bread and *foul* beans bought from a stall on the way to work. We then have a bigger snack for morning tea. Lunch is usually bread and cheese, or rice with meat and a salad. Cooked meat and rice, or stew with bread, is served for the main evening meal. This is often followed by fruit such as watermelon. More tasty snacks are eaten for supper at around 10 p.m.

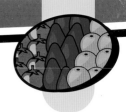

A woman baking bread in a dome-shaped oven, known as a taboon.

Many of our dishes, such as a spicy dip called *baba ghannooj,* are made with eggplant. Okra, chick peas, sesame seeds and *foul* beans are also popular ingredients. My favourite dish is felafel, deep-fried balls made from chick peas and crushed wheat. I also love to eat *bassboussa,* a sweet cake made from yoghurt and semolina. It is smothered in sugary syrup. Yum!

Our markets are known as souks. They are the best place to buy meat, spices, and fresh fruit and vegetables.

Make hommos

Egyptian people usually start their main meal with several small dishes such as hommos, spicy eggplant dip, and tahini (a paste made from ground sesame seeds). These are served with flat bread.

Ask an adult to help you prepare this dish.

You will need:

- 2 cups chick peas, cooked
- 1 large clove garlic
- 2 tablespoons tahini paste
- 1/4 cup cold water
- juice of 1/2 lemon
- salt and pepper
- a blender or food processor

What to do:

1 Place all the ingredients into a blender or food processor.

2 Blend until the mixture is smooth and creamy.

3 Serve with Arabic flat bread that has been warmed in the oven.

The ancient Egyptians did not have an alphabet with 26 letters. Instead, they wrote using picture symbols called hieroglyphics. There were over 700 different symbols. Some of the symbols stood for whole words, and others for only one or two letters. Messages were written on long scrolls of 'paper' made from **papyrus**.

You will need:

- a pen or marker
- a long, thick piece of paper
- a strip of ribbon or raffia

What to do:

1 Write a message to a friend using some of the symbols on this page. Bunch the symbols together in groups. (The Egyptians did not use full stops.)

2 Roll up the piece of paper and tie it with the ribbon or raffia.

3 Give the scroll to your friend.

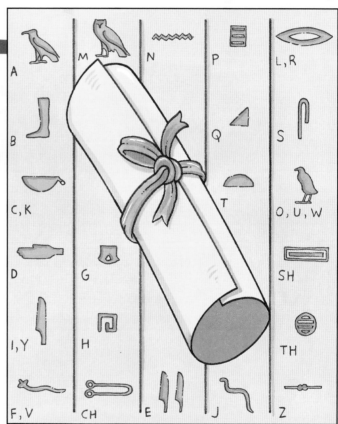

Landscape and climate

Egypt is shaped like a square, with a triangle tacked onto the side. The triangular part is known as the Sinai **Peninsula**. There are three main types of landscapes in Egypt – dry desert regions, the rich and green lands of the Nile Valley, and mountainous areas in the south and on the Sinai Peninsula.

The Western Desert covers two-thirds of the country. The sand dunes here can be 200 metres high and 100 kilometres long. The wind blows them into different places and shapes. Sometimes they cover roads or swallow up whole villages. Temperatures in the desert range from 46°C during summer days, to below freezing on winter nights.

Feluccas on the River Nile. The Nile flows through Egypt for 1545 kilometres, but its total length is 6671 kilometres. This makes it the longest river in the world. The Nile flows from the south to the north, and empties into the Mediterranean Sea.

*The land in the Nile Valley is good for growing crops. About 90 per cent of Egyptian people live in the Nile Valley or **delta** region.*

The dry desert land of the Sinai Peninsula. The northern part of the peninsula is dry and sandy, while the south is more mountainous. The granite mountain range found here includes Gebel Katherina (Mount Catherine). It is 2642 metres tall, the highest peak in Egypt. The tops of this range are covered by snow in winter.

Average temperatures

	January	July
Cairo	14°C	28°C
Aswan	17°C	34°C
Alexandria	15°C	27°C
Siwa	12°C	30°C

Egypt hardly ever gets any rain, or even clouds. In Cairo, there are usually only five days of rain each year. Here in Siwa, we get rain only once or twice every 100 years!

Plants and animals

Date palms grow throughout the delta region, in the Nile Valley, and around the oases in the desert. Other native trees include acacias, eucalypts and sycamores. Coarse alfa grass, tamarisks, and thorny shrubs and herbs grow in desert areas.

During the time of the **pharaohs**, there were ostriches, crocodiles, hippopotamuses and giraffes living along the Nile. As more people came to live here, these animals slowly died out. Gazelles, jackals and hyenas still live in the desert, and there are small numbers of boar, lynx and wildcats in the delta region.

We have 33 different types of snakes, including the Egyptian cobra, the horned viper and the hooded snake. There are also scorpions, lizards and scarab beetles. Many storks, ducks and other **migratory birds** use our lakes as feeding grounds.

There are 30 different types of date palms found growing throughout Egypt.

Camels have adapted brilliantly to life in the desert, where there is little food or water. They can drink around 100 litres of water at once, then go for days without drinking.

The coral reef in the Red Sea is home to many colourful fish, as well as tiger sharks and moray eels. There are many hotels and ships in the south Sinai area. The Ras Mohammed Marine National Park helps to protect the coral and fish from their pollution and **sewage**.

A long-nosed hawkfish swims through coral on Thomas Reef in the Red Sea.

Cities and landmarks

About half of our people live in towns and cities. Half of these city-dwellers live in our capital city, Cairo. It is the largest city by population on the African continent, having over 15 million people. Cairo is a mixture of the old and the new. Ancient mosques and bustling bazaars (markets) sit next to modern office blocks and apartment buildings. On the edge of the city are the massive pyramids, built by the ancient Egyptians.

The city of Cairo. Its large population and huge amount of traffic have brought many problems, including air pollution.

Alexandria, on the north Mediterranean coast, is our second-largest city. It was founded by Alexander the Great. In ancient times, Alexandria was the capital city, and Cleopatra reigned here as queen. These days, the city is an important harbour and centre for industry. Other major cities are Aswan, Port Said and Suez.

One of the three pyramids at Giza, near Cairo. There were Seven Wonders of the Ancient World. The Great Pyramid of Khufu is the only one of the Seven Wonders that is still standing.

Tourists come from all over the world to visit our many historic sites and monuments. The most important of these are at Karnak, Abu Simbel, Sakkara, Memphis, Giza, and Luxor, which is part of the ancient City of Thebes.

The Avenue of Sphinxes at the Temple of Karnak, north of Luxor. This huge complex includes temples dedicated to the god Amun-Re and his wife Mut. Sphinxes were mythological creatures with the body of a lion and a human head. They stood for strength and wisdom.

Industry and agriculture

Our major industries include food processing and textiles. We have several large cement, fertiliser and aluminium plants. Iron ore is mined in the Western Desert. It provides the raw material for our iron- and steel-processing industries. Oil was first discovered here in 1938. It is an increasingly important part of our economy. The main oilfields are located in the Gulf of Suez. There are also natural gas fields at Abu Gharadiq and Abu Madi.

Tourism is vital to our economy. Back in the days of steamship travel, many passengers sailed through the Suez Canal on their way to and from Europe. They would stop in Egypt to visit the pyramids, travelling by camel or donkey. The trip took a full day. These days, people are more likely to travel by luxury bus. Tourists crowd our wonderful museums and historic monuments. Many of them also visit Sinai to go snorkelling and diving in the Red Sea.

Men work on an offshore oil-drilling platform near Abu Rudeis.

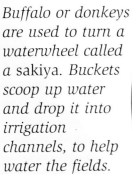

Buffalo or donkeys are used to turn a waterwheel called a sakiya. Buckets scoop up water and drop it into irrigation channels, to help water the fields.

Most farms are located along the Nile delta or valley. Our major crops are cotton, rice, maize, wheat, clover and beans. Sugarcane is grown in Upper Egypt. Because it hardly ever rains in Egypt, the farmers must **irrigate** the land.

Many Egyptians are too poor to own modern farm machinery. Instead, they work their fields by hand.

Transport

About 10 per cent of Egyptian families own cars, and over half of these people live in our main cities. It costs a lot of money to import cars. That is why most of our cars are very old – especially our taxis! There are over 64 000 kilometres of highways, although only three-quarters of our roads are paved. Major highways connect Cairo with the cities of Alexandria, Port Said, Suez and Fayoum.

Around 10 million people in Egypt use public transport every day. Luxury air-conditioned buses are used by tourists, but most of our buses are very old and in poor condition. Our railway system is one of the oldest in the region. There are nearly 5000 kilometres of track.

The streets of Cairo are jammed with cars and buses. This causes a major pollution problem.

Our main ports are at Alexandria, Port Said and Suez. The Suez Canal is a waterway that was built to link the Mediterranean with the Red Sea. It is wide and deep enough to allow ocean-going ships to travel along it. The Canal was closed between 1967 and 1975 during the Arab–Israeli war. There are over 90 airfields in the country. Our national airline is Egypt Air.

A crowded passenger ferry on the Nile at Luxor. There are 3500 kilometres of waterways in Egypt. Many people use these to travel around the country.

In the desert, sometimes a donkey is the only means of transport available. Some people use camels – including the police and postal workers.

History and government

People first began living along the Nile around 5000 years ago. As the population grew, the many small villages grouped together to form two strong kingdoms. These were the Kingdom of Upper Egypt in the Nile Valley, and the Kingdom of Lower Egypt in the delta. Eventually, a powerful king named Narmer united the two kingdoms to form the first **dynasty**.

Kings ruled Egypt for the next 3000 years. They were known as pharaohs, and they left behind huge structures called pyramids. The pharaohs believed that, after they died, their bodies would be kept safe in the pyramids. Each pharaoh tried to outdo the one before him, making his own pyramid much bigger and grander. One king, Snefou, even built two pyramids!

The Great Sphinx and the Pyramid of Khafre at Giza. Khafre was a pharaoh from a period known as the Old Kingdom. The Sphinx was cut from a natural outcrop of limestone during the fourth dynasty.

A stone carving of the Pharaoh Akhenaton and Nefertiti at the Egyptian Museum in Cairo. After Akhenaton's death, a new king named Tutankhamun came to the throne. He was only 10 years old. In 1922, his magnificent tomb was discovered buried deep in the Valley of the Kings by Howard Carter, an English archaeologist.

The reign of the pharaohs ended when Egypt was invaded by the Assyrians in 671 BC. Other cultures arrived over the next several hundred years. These included the Nubians, Persians, Greeks and Romans. Egypt became a Christian country around AD 500, but fell to the Arabs in AD 639. Gradually, the people began to speak Arabic and follow the Muslim religion.

Egypt then became part of several different European **empires**, including the British Empire. The country gained independence in 1922, but British troops did not leave until 1947. In 1952, a revolution overthrew the reigning king, who was sent into exile.

These days Egypt is a republic. It is ruled by a president, who is also head of the armed forces. All adults must vote in the elections. The government is working hard to achieve a better standard of living for our people.

Fact file

Official name Arab Republic of Egypt		**Population** 68 000 000	**Land area** 1 001 450 square kilometres
Government republic	**Languages** Arabic (official), English, French		**Religions** Islam (mostly Sunni), Christianity (Coptic)
Currency Egyptian pound (E£) 1 Egyptian pound = 100 piastres		**Capital city** Cairo	**Major cities** Alexandria, Port Said, Suez
		**Climate** hot, dry summers and mild winters	
Major river Nile		**Length of coastline** 2450 kilometres	**Highest mountain** Mount Catherine (2637 metres)
Main farm products cotton, rice, corn, wheat, beans, fruit, vegetables, cattle, water buffalo, sheep, goats, fish	**Main industries** textiles, food processing, tourism, chemicals, petroleum, construction, cement, metals		**Natural resources** petroleum, natural gas, iron ore, phosphates, limestone, talc, asbestos, lead, zinc

Glossary

Bedouin	Arab tribes of the desert who move around in search of food, instead of living in one place
Berber	the language of the Berbers, a tribal people of North Africa
delta	a fan-shaped area of land at the mouth of a river, where it divides into many small branches that flow into the sea
dynasty	a series of rulers who are from the same family
empire	a group of countries that is controlled by one ruler or government
feluccas	long, narrow boats
irrigate	to provide water for fields using a series of channels and pipes
Islam	the Muslim religion, based on Mohammed's teachings about the one god, Allah
Mecca	a city in Saudi Arabia where the prophet Mohammed was born. It is considered the holiest city in Islam
migratory birds	birds that travel from one part of the world to another when the seasons change
mother-of-pearl	the pink-white shiny material found inside pearl oyster shells
oasis	a rich, green part of the desert that is watered by a spring, stream or well
papyrus	a water reed used for making paper
peninsula	an area of land, often narrow, that juts out from the mainland
pharaohs	ancient Egyptian kings
prophet	a teacher or leader who claims to speak to God or Allah
Ramadan	the ninth month of the Muslim year, a holy month when people fast and pray
sewage	waste matter that is carried away in special pipes

Index

	Page
agriculture	25
Alexandria	6, 9, 19, 22, 26, 27
ancient Egypt	10, 11, 12, 22, 28–29
animals	20–21
Bedouin	6, 14
Berber	5, 6
Cairo	6, 9, 11, 12, 13, 19, 22, 23, 26, 29
climate	18–19
culture	10–11
deserts	5, 18, 19, 20, 21, 24, 27
family life	6–7
festivals	12–13
flag	4, 5
food	14–15, 16
government	29
hieroglyphics	11, 17
history	28–29
housing	6
Howard Carter	29
industry	24–25

	Page
landscape	18–19
Luxor	10, 23, 27
Mecca	12
Mohammed	5, 12
Mount Catherine	19
Nile Valley	18, 19, 20, 25, 28
plants	20
pyramids	22, 23, 28, 29
Red Sea	5, 21, 24, 27
religion	5, 8, 12–13, 29
rivers	5, 9, 18, 27
school	8
Siwa	5, 6, 19
sport	9
Suez Canal	24, 27
transport	24, 26–27
Tutankhamun	29
writers	11

Charles R. Beaudoin Public School
4313 Clubview Drive
Burlington, Ontario